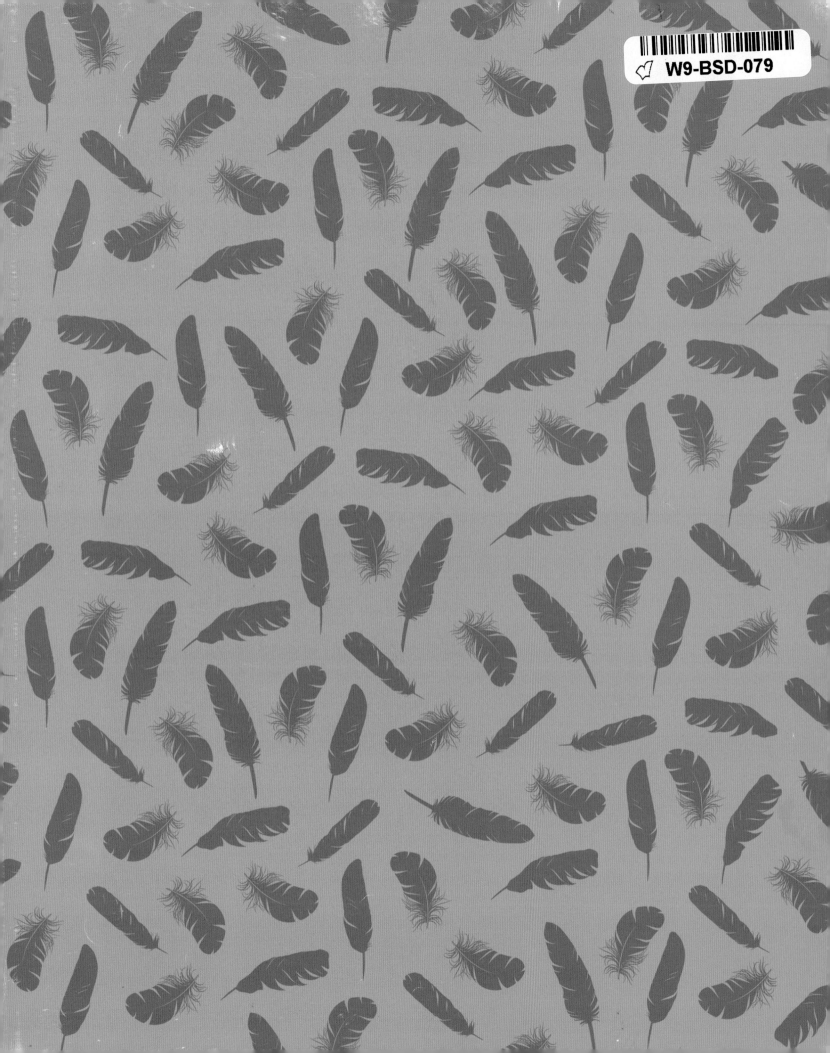

For my parents, Paul and Charlene Sultan,
who created the best nest ever
—J. W.

For Robin
—S. J.

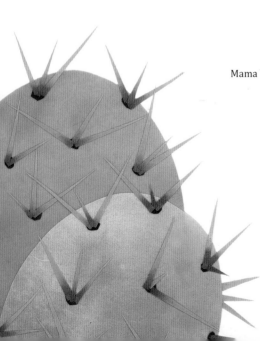

BEACH LANE BOOKS
An imprint of Simon & Schuster Children's Publishing Division
1230 Avenue of the Americas, New York, New York 10020
Text copyright © 2014 by Jennifer Ward
Illustrations copyright © 2014 by Steve Jenkins
All rights reserved, including the right of reproduction in whole or in part in any form.
BEACH LANE BOOKS is a trademark of Simon & Schuster, Inc.
For information about special discounts for bulk purchases,
please contact Simon & Schuster Special Sales
at 1-866-506-1949 or business@simonandschuster.com.
The Simon & Schuster Speakers Bureau can bring authors to your live event. For more
information or to book an event, contact the Simon & Schuster Speakers Bureau
at 1-866-248-3049 or visit our website at www.simonspeakers.com.
Book design by Sonia Chaghatzbanian
The text for this book is set in Cambria and Century Gothic.
The illustrations for this book are collage.
Manufactured in China
1213 SCP
First Edition
2 4 6 8 10 9 7 5 3 1
Library of Congress Cataloging-in-Publication Data
Ward, Jennifer.
Mama built a little nest / Jennifer Ward ; illustrated by Steve Jenkins.—First edition.
p. cm.
ISBN 978-1-4424-2116-5 (hardcover)
ISBN 978-1-4424-4945-9 (eBook)
1. Birds—Nests—Juvenile literature. 2. Birds—Juvenile literature.
I. Jenkins, Steve, 1952– illustrator. II. Title.
QL676.2.W382 2014
598.156'4—dc23
2013003343

Jennifer Ward illustrated by Steve Jenkins

Mama built a little nest

Beach Lane Books
New York London Toronto Sydney New Delhi

Mama built a little nest
inside a sturdy trunk.
She used her beak to *tap-tap-tap*
the perfect place to bunk.

Tree-hole nests, also known as cavity nests, are created by the male and female woodpecker.

Mama built a little nest,
a cup so wee and snug,
with walls of moss and roof of sky
and silky, cobweb rug.

A hummingbird makes the
smallest cup-shaped nest.
It uses spiderweb
so the little nest will stretch
as the chicks grow.

Mama built a little nest.
Well, actually, she didn't.
She found one that another made,
and then she laid me in it.

Not all birds build nests. The cowbird, whydah, and cuckoo find a nest built by another bird species. They lay their eggs in it and fly off, leaving their eggs in the care of the bird who built the nest.

Mama built a little nest.
My daddy helped out too.
They placed my egg upon his feet.
That's where I hatched and grew.

The emperor penguin uses a living nest: the father penguin. The father uses his beak to roll the mother's egg upon his feet quickly, so it doesn't freeze, and carefully, so it doesn't break. There it stays buried under his tummy folds for about sixty days, warm and protected.

Mama scraped a simple nest
upon a craggy ledge.
She tucked me safe within her wings
until my time to fledge.

Certain birds, such as the falcon, create a nest, called a scrape, on a high cliff edge. The mother and father may scrape away at the ledge, creating a small indentation.

Daddy built a little nest.
And then he built another.
And another. And another—
hoping to impress my mother.

Like many wrens, a male cactus wren builds several dome-shaped nests to attract a female. If impressed, the female will choose one and then continue to add to its structure. Remaining nests may be used as resting places (roosts) by the father and may also serve as decoys to confuse predators.

Mama built a little nest.
She used her beak to sew
a woven nest of silky grass,
the perfect place to grow.

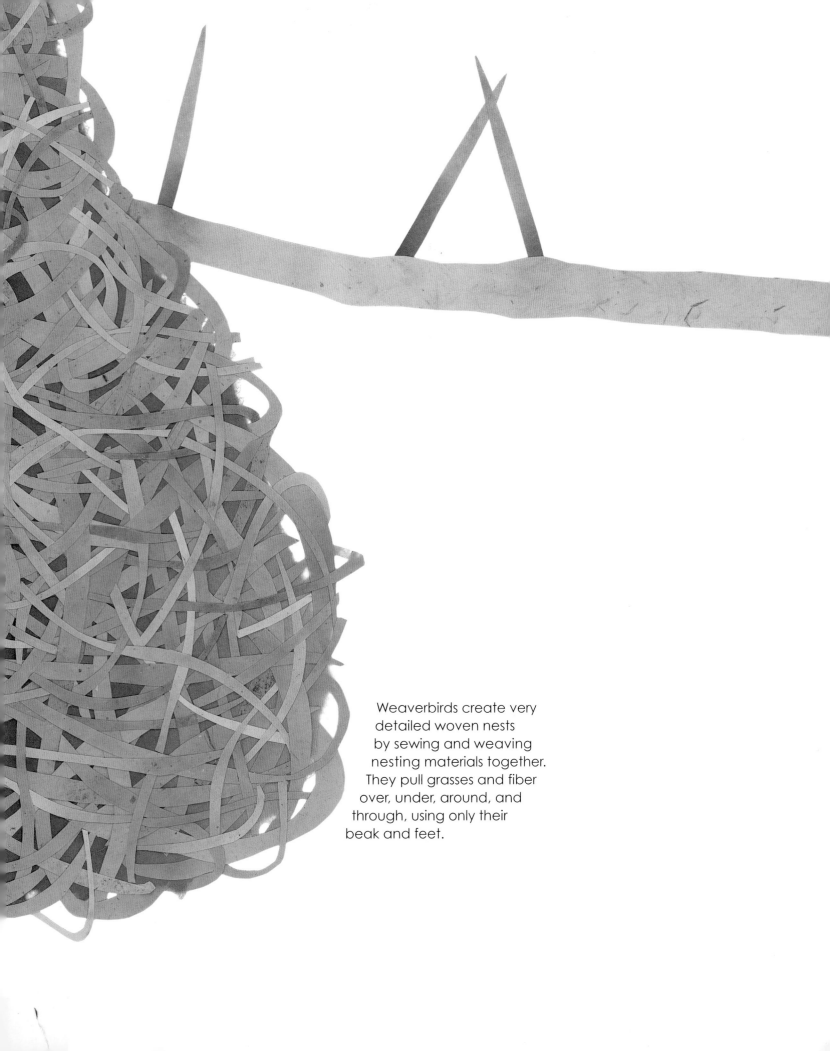

Weaverbirds create very
detailed woven nests
by sewing and weaving
nesting materials together.
They pull grasses and fiber
over, under, around, and
through, using only their
beak and feet.

Mama built a little nest
by digging out a burrow.
It was a hoot, our little home,
a safe and feathery furrow.

The burrowing owl nests underground in a burrow nest. It can dig its own burrow, or use an abandoned burrow created by a mammal.

Mama built a little nest.
She gathered twigs that float
and placed them on the water
to create a cozy boat.

Grebes create a floating nest on the water and anchor it to water plants.

Mama built a little nest.
She made it on the ground.
A simple nest, not very soft,
with pebbles, smooth and round.

Many shorebirds create scrape nests on the ground. Their eggs often have colors and patterns to help camouflage them with their environment. Can you find the eggs in this picture?

Daddy built a little nest—
now don't gross out—with spit.
Who would have thought that spit would make
the perfect place to sit?

The swiftlet makes an edible nest using tube-shaped saliva, which hardens in the air. Swiftlet nests are used in bird's nest soup, a Chinese delicacy.

Mama built a sealed nest
within an old tree's hollow.
My daddy left a little hole
to pass her food to swallow.

The hornbill makes a cavity nest
inside a tree hollow. With the
female inside and the male outside,
both birds use mud and droppings
to seal the cavity. A small hole is left
open, which the male uses to feed the
female. She remains locked inside the nest
to incubate their clutch. After the chicks have
hatched, the female breaks out, helping the
male feed and care for their young from the outside
until the chicks are old enough to leave the nest.

Mama built a sturdy nest
by stacking twigs up high—
a breezy house upon a tree,
where talons blend with sky.

The male and female bald eagle build a stick nest, called an aerie, by gathering and layering many sticks. Their nests are among the largest of all bird nests, usually five to six feet in diameter and two to four feet high.

Mama built a little nest
entirely out of mud.
No feathery down, no soft green plants,
just fuddy, muddy crud.

The male and female flamingo build a mound-shaped nest on the ground using mud, into which the female lays just one egg.

You have a nest—your very own!
A place to rest your head
with pillows soft and cozy thoughts—

your nest is called a bed.

A note from the author

I've always been a birder, but many years ago when a hummingbird built her wee *cup* nest atop a mobile hanging outside my kitchen window, it made me wonder. I couldn't help but marvel at the remarkable ingenuity behind the architectural process (it took that hummingbird two weeks to assemble her little nest!) and at the wide range of nests birds create.

Birds are skilled, inventive, and adaptable builders. Nest design may be minimal (as with a *scrape*) or mind-bogglingly intricate (as with a *woven*). Size may be tiny (*hummingbird*) or huge (*eagle*). Birds design *burrow*, *cavity*, and *mound* nests. They sew and craft *woven*, *dome*, and *hanging* nests. They produce nests that float, defy gravity, expand, are camouflaged, and that heat or cool. Indeed, these avian architects create the most varied type of home of any wild species, allowing them to live in a diversity of habitats. In dry deserts and rainy forests, upon open groundscapes and open water, high in the sky and under the ground, within urban spaces and in the wild, birds and their nests can be found everywhere across the globe. And perhaps most amazingly, birds construct these artful, brilliantly engineered nests with nary a finger or opposable thumb to help them.

Birds and their nests—aren't they *marvelous*?

Resources for further learning and exploration:

American Birding Association: aba.org
American Ornithologists' Union: aou.org
National Audubon Society: audubon.org
Avibase: avibase.bsc-eoc.org
Cornell Lab of Ornithology: birds.cornell.edu
NestWatch: nestwatch.org